# HOLIDAYS 2000
## A TIME CAPSULE

Ian Moncrief-Scott

Information Management Solutions Limited

ISLE OF MAN

The author Ian Moncrief-Scott has asserted his right under the Copyright, Designs and Patents Act 1988 to be identified as the author of this work.

Copyright. © I. Moncrief-Scott 2021

All rights reserved. No part of this publication may be produced in any form or by any means - graphic, electronic, or mechanical, including photocopying, recording, taping, or information storage and retrieval systems - without the prior permission in writing of the publishers.

The publishers make no representation, express or implied, regarding the accuracy of the information contained in this book and cannot accept any legal responsibility for any errors or omissions that may take place.

A CIP catalogue record for this book is available from the British Library.

Published by Information Management Solutions Limited, 17 Howe Road, Onchan, Isle of Man, IM3 2BB.

Printed, bound and distributed by IngramSpark.

Book Layout © 2017 BookDesignTemplates.com

**HOLIDAYS 2000: A TIME CAPSULE - 2nd ed.**
ISBN 9781903467213

The Publishers have been requested by the author to acknowledge the direct and indirect contributions to this book by:

Yorkshire Tourist Board
Gibraltar Tourist Board
Greek National Tourism Organisation
Atlanta Convention & Visitors Bureau

**The Publishers have been further requested by the author to advise readers that this is a second edition that mirrors the original one by a different publisher but maintains the time capsule principle of the year 2000, though some individual venues may have changed.**

This book is dedicated to
start-up entrepreneurs.


The front cover depicts
ordinary wooden clothes pegs dressed as
Super Heroes.


**All start-up entrepreneurs are
ordinary people
turning into Super Heroes!**

# CONTENTS

**FIRST STOP YORK** ............................................................... 1
**MARRIAGE ON THE ROCK** .................................................. 9
**THE OTHER EMERALD ISLE** ............................................. 15
**MALLS & FALLS** ................................................................ 21
**OTHER BOOKS BY THE AUTHOR (Print)** ........................ 27
**OTHER BOOKS BY THE AUTHOR (eBook)** ..................... 28
**NEW EDITIONS & FORTHCOMING BOOKS BY THE AUTHOR** ................................................................................ 29

CHAPTER ONE

# FIRST STOP YORK

Ever since the Vikings discovered they could have a great time, York has welcomed visitors.

Sheltered from the extremes of the British winter, the City has become a favourite year-round attraction. Not that bad weather need be a problem. Indoor entertainment is plentiful and high street shopping compact, yet extensive. York's excellent road, rail, and coach links provide an ideal base to explore Yorkshire, largest county in the United Kingdom.

Walking the characteristic Yorkshire stonewalls that almost totally surround the City is a perfect way to reach your chosen attraction. You don't have to be as fit as the Roman slaves who built them but it does take over two hours to stroll their entire length.

Just twenty steps reach the parapets. Above the hustle and bustle powerfully reminds you of the days when the fortress could only be breached by the Bars at each corner.

March and April announce the Celebration of Daffodils when the grassy banks below the walls strikingly contrast a mass of golden flowers.

Castle Museum is an absolute 'must'. Wandering through cobbled streets and venturing into the prison cell of notorious highwayman, Dick Turpin, you can sense him yell, "Stand and Deliver!" Take a break and swing into the 60's coffee bar, full of Rock and Roll memories.

Across the road is York Dungeon, where beheading and drowning are common. Don't be afraid to scream-you won't be alone! Beware-York's infamous Guy Fawkes is trying to blow up the Houses of Parliament.

A short walk down Castlegate draws you to a unique adventure at the world famous, Jorvik Viking Centre. Step aboard a Time Car and travel backwards to witness, taste and smell history.

If you are lucky to visit in February, the Annual Viking Festival will appeal. Colourful longships race along the River Ouse.

Combat displays, saga telling and ancient music, culminate in a spectacular boat-burning finale.

Turning out of Coppergate, a few steps finds you in the narrow streets, and overhanging shops, of the Shambles. Step back and imagine life in earlier centuries, with merchants plying their trade. Buy a souvenir or pop into the adjacent open air market.

For a break, take a seat in Parliament Square. Feed the pigeons. Marvel at the skills of street entertainers, or simply relax, and people-watch. This is a focus of retail shopping. Cars are prohibited and pavements lowered to make walking safe and easy. Almost every high street store is represented, Virgin Megastore, M&S, C&A and, of course, Disney, with its own brand of magic.

Leading up from Stonegate, with its array of fine shops is York Minster and St. William's College-visible thirty miles from the City. It is the largest medieval church north of the Alps with a wealth of stained glass, mostly original. Gaze at the famous Rose window, miraculously surviving a massive fire, which destroyed the entire North precept. Donations from across the globe have aided restoration.

July sees the Early Music Festival in a wide variety of medieval churches, historic houses and ancient guildhalls. Evening concerts by candlelight, afternoon lectures and illustrated walks animate the events.

Full steam ahead for a 'Brief Encounter' at the National Railway Museum. Bells ringing, a mini-train shuttles you over Lendal Bridge. Re-live two hundred years of railway life. See the palaces on wheels. Emulate the footsteps of King George V and Queen Mary, on the sumptuous red carpet. Smile with Thomas the Tank Engine. On weekends, actors bring the trains to life.

All this fun gives you an appetite. There's plenty of choice. Silver service at Betty's Tea Rooms, pizzas at Silvano's and, of course, MacDonalds. Romantics might prefer Casa Alberto or Meltons, the Consumers Association Good Food Guide's 'Restaurant of the Year.'

Quenching your thirst is easy. York boasts a pub for each day of the year, and York Brewery, welcomes you to its showcase. Don't get too drunk you might miss a ghostly encounter in a snickleway or a snug.

For the really 'famished and parched', the Annual Food and Drink Festival in September is the solution. Celebrate international cuisine in a variety of venues across the City.

What better way to let your refreshment settle than 'Cruising the Ouse.' Fully guided leisure trips sail hourly or hire a private day boat. Voyage down past York Racecourse to Bishopthorpe Palace, the home of the Archbishop, and on to a well-deserved G&T at the Ship Inn at Acaster. Sailing upstream? See the flood barrier, vital for preventing the tidal Ouse watering the drinks at the Kings Arms on the banks of the river.

Thirty to sixty minutes by car or train from York extends your entertainment options. Nauticals would appreciate vibrant Scarborough, quaint Whitby (famous for Captain Cook), and picturesque Robin Hood's Bay can be found easily. Castle Howard's splendid gardens and rooms are well worth a small detour. If crossing the North York Moors National Park, visit the Steam Railway or, the nearby set of TV's Heartbeat. Picnic in Pickering or see Flamingoland Adventure Park.

Should military matters appeal, Yorkshire Air Museum at Elvington, an operational airfield, has Halifax and Mosquito rebuilds, and Victor tanker 'Lusty Lindy'. Have a drink in the NAAFI, and visit the authentically restored Flying Control Tower.

Leeds presents The Royal Armouries, Britain's largest postwar leisure development and, arguably, the most exciting. Five themed galleries of Tournament, Self-Defence, War, Hunting, and the Orient, bring history to life with latest interactive technology. While inside, you can savour the extraordinary atmosphere of everything from an Edwardian Gunroom to a Japanese Tea Garden. A remarkable day out.

The Army Museum, Beverley, and Eden WW II camp, Malton, the only theme museum of its type in the world, will let you experience the sights, sounds and even smells of those dangerous years.

Nostell Priory, Fountains Abbey, Rievaulx Abbey, Benningborough Hall, Brimham Rocks, and the towns of Harrogate and Knaresborough all add colour and culture.

Accommodation is plentiful in York. Guest houses nestle comfortably alongside major hotel chains. You might manage a quick round of golf at Alwark Manor or the luxury at Middlethorpe Hall.

Park and Ride facilities at most City entrances and Tourist Information Points help plan your adventure.

So much to do, so little time, aptly describes the City of York. See how much you can do? Make it First Stop York!

CHAPTER TWO

# MARRIAGE ON THE ROCK

Sean Connery married twice. John Lennon and Yoko Ono wed there. Knot-tying is one of Gibraltar's offshore secrets.

A brief telephone call to the friendly staff at the Registry set our date. You don't even have to stay on the Island. Though, The Rock, is an hypnotic and imposing umpire to the azure waters of the Mediterranean and the crashing ebony tides of the Atlantic.

In stark contrast to the conveyor-belt weddings of the Caribbean, the Authorities only allow three ceremonies daily to guarantee your day remains special.

We obtained the non-residents' Governor's Special Licence the day before. We needed an affidavit, confirming our freedom to marry but a walk to a local solicitor or commissioner for oaths, dealt with this promptly and cheaply.

Remember to take your original birth certificate, degree absolute and any statutory declaration or deed poll changes. Don't forget your passport and the marriage fee!

In the modest Registry, the ceremony is traditional and very dignified. Proceedings are conducted in English, though Gibraltarians are equally at home with Spanish. Your guests are very welcome and video cameras allowed. However, flash photography must wait until the vows have been completed.

The Registry and its adjacent Courthouse, make picturesque and convenient backdrops for recording the occasion. The shell mosaic gardens and black iron railings afford essential sanctuary from the intense summer heat and bustling city centre traffic. Please throw environmentally-friendly confetti!

Ample accommodation is available on the compact Island. Around from Main Street, Elliots, the former White's Hotel, is the most sophisticated. For those on a tighter budget, try the Bristol across the road. Both the beach-fronted Hotel Caleta Palace and the Rock Hotel's tropical gardens yield a more tranquil setting.

We stayed at the magnificent all-inclusive four-star Hotel Reina Cristina, in Spain's nearby Algeciras, with its attractive and expansive walled gardens. An ideal venue for photographs.

Staying off the Island gives a more eventful and memorable start to your Special Day. Arrival by car or coach is erratic and unpredictable. Border crossing delays can vary from thirty minutes to three hours.

Help is at hand. Spanish taxis drive to the front of the queue. So why not join the intrepid, who walked across the border, passport in hand, in full regalia, to smiles and cheers from both sides. A Gibraltarian limousine, or taxi can collect you on the other side less than 50 yards away!

Entertaining your guests is easy. Take the cable car to reach the world-famous Barbary Apes, in the Nature Reserve. Legend says if they leave, The Rock will cease to be British. Their colonies are expanding.

St. Michael's cave offers spectacular natural grottoes, culminating in a massive underground lake, forming a magnificent natural auditorium. The haunting tunes of the musicians, serenading from rowing boats, impinge long after the sunlight awakens your pupils.

Important military and strategic heritage is everywhere. From Nelson's final Trafalgar journey to 34 amazing miles of access and defence tunnels, blasted by the Royal Engineers, deep inside the tiny 2.5 square mile Island.

Relax, watching the hundreds of varied craft sailing the Straights or navigating the modern Marina. Charter a boat to see the dolphins, or the dramatic Spanish, Portuguese and Moroccan coastlines, clambering from the sea.

Shopping facilities are home from home and include Marks & Spencer, British Home Stores and thinking ahead, Mothercare. All easily accessible on the pedestrianised, narrow Main Street.

You will be delighted to learn that no **V**AT ensures cheap duty - free goods. Stylish Gibraltar crystal is great value and watching it being made adds charm.

Getting to The Rock is easy with direct frequent flights, short-breaks and holidays from leading UK airports.

Gibraltar is truly international and proudly British. So why not join Tony Jacklin, Des O'Connor, Peter de Savary, Frederick Forsyth and Simon Bates in a wedding with a difference?

CHAPTER THREE

# THE OTHER EMERALD ISLE

Thassos is different. Its Eric Cantona is different. Its Vagis museum is different. Termed the 'Other Emerald Isle', set in a sapphire Aegean Sea, you will find it languishing beneath the Macedonian coast of Greece and nearby rival, Turkey.

We arrived at the cramped Kevala airport on the mainland and after trusting our luggage to a vintage open truck, the short ferry ride provided an early glimpse of sanctuary.

Disembarking at Limenas gives you the first hint that Thassos is different. For a capital it is quiet. No bustle. The pace is soporific. A few indistinct tavernas line the harbour. Colourful boats, equipped with searchlights for night fishing, pulsate nonchalantly in the crystaline waters, undisturbed by time. Mildly curious locals stare over their raki and coffee. Only the occasional rumble of a lorry straining under a massive marble block, freshly hewn from the nearby white mountains, punctuates the serenity.

We made Skala Potomia our base. A wise choice. Surging 1208m skywards, Mount Hypsarion strikes a magnificent rugged backdrop to the golden beach. Once a mere thoroughfare to the shimmering sea, a sprinkling of fine tavernas now decorate the shoreline. Enticing you to relax, inviting terraces bridle the beating sun with their broad-leaved vines, heavy with fruit.

Our host explained, "My ancestors came down from our main village, Potomia, to harvest prawns and catch red snapper. Pirates made it perilous to live on the coast. Now we have friendly invaders, mainly from Greece." Adding the finishing touches to a Greek salad she continued, "Sixteen years ago, we opened for twenty days a season. Then one month, gradually two, three. Now we spend six months here. When our guests disappear in October, as the weather becomes unsettled, we wish them a 'good winter', and return to our homes. About a metre of snow lands on the beach in January, but gathering grapes, making wine and collecting olives soon brings next May."

For an unusual eatery try Avalon. Formerly, a derelict fishing refuge, where monks slept on the mezzanine floor above their boats, it has been sympathetically revived. Giant pizza fired outside in the woodburning oven, or succulent lamb from the grill, plus a carafe of red wine, will leave two of you change from €10.00.

Comfortable accommodation is dotted around the village. Rooms cost as little as €20 per week. We found the Nama and neighbouring Barbara apartments excellent value with characteristically friendly hosts. If you have a larger budget, the Blue Bay hotel, a Thomson Gold award winner for three years, perched at the far end of the beach, dispenses a spectacular panoramic view. Not for the vertigo challenged, but worth the trek.

Eric Cantona is alive, healthy and running his taverna in Thassos. Well, not exactly. Stratos Papafilipou is the spitting image of the former Manchester United star and a truly charming man to boot. Two years ago, a visitor pointed out the uncanny resemblance. Stratos and his Eric's bar have never looked back.

Rising out of the morning mist shrouding the verdant pines, you can make out the parental village of Potomia, birthplace of Polygnotos Vagis, internationally acclaimed artist and sculptor. his museum displays some fine works. Not secured in glass cabinets but in true Thassian style, on open view for you to enjoy the sensations.

We were honoured by an unexpected invitation to a christening. At birth, Greek children do not receive a first name. Chosen by the 'best children', the name is conferred by the priest while the father waits anxiously outside the church. All the youngsters run to tell the father, who rewards them with small gifts and sweets.

You cannot miss a visit to Panagia with its whitewashed, slate roof cottages. The women of the village, possibly the earliest female DIY experts, insist that they, not their husbands, repaint the external walls every few months. Welcome a refreshing drink in the village plaza where, yearlong, three chilling mountain streams converge into intriguing open channels, before cascading into miniature waterfalls. At the edge of the lower village, a house dating back to 1642 survives, its narrow ground floor slits testament to attentions of unwanted marauders. Take a few minutes to see the small church, with its Crusader banner presented by Richard the Lionheart.

A visit to Phillippi on the mainland is an absolute must. We took an official tour that you will find essential to fully appreciate the ancient city. Approaching Phillipii on the Via Egnatia, the route of the original Roman road, you will be impressed by the scale of the city. Stretching as far as the eye can see, boundaried only by mountain ranges.

Leading down through the Roman cemetery you will find yourself beside the rushing water, where almost two thousand years ago, St. Paul baptised the first Christian, Lydia.

The ruins of the city are everywhere. Our guide, Angela, a qualified archaeologist, gained us special permission to see the latest discoveries. The earliest known Christian church in the world, built in 313AD, has just been revealed.

We marvelled at the marks ground into the hard marble road by chariot wheels, the scene of the decisive battle for the Roman empire between Brutus and Casius against Mark Antony and Octavius in 42BC.

Across the busy road stand two Basilicas and the amphitheatre. Angela explained, "The Romans removed the first two rows of marble seating from the original Greek theatre to erect security walls so that gladiators, lions and Christians could entertain the spectators in relative safety."

A word of warning for those travelling in October. Thassos is world famous for its honey, especially its pine honey. At this time of the year, keepers turn out their hives ready for the winter. Billions of bees search for a new home. Leeming-like they head for the beach, a constant threat to your exposed feet.

We journeyed home with RSI - repetitive swat injury, but cannot wait to return to this accessible couples' sanctuary next spring.

.

CHAPTER FOUR

# MALLS & FALLS

After threatening deportation and exacting $170 for a media visa waiver, the Atlanta Immigration Officer could not have been more helpful. "You must go to Stone Mountain Park and Buckhead," urged the impromptu tourist guru.

I warmed up with Scorcher, Six Flags Over Georgia's newest addition to MindBender and Great American Scream Machine. Standing at 54 mph in a purple and gold rollercoaster bucking 3000feet of contorted rails does little to settle your breakfast but greatly improves your circulation.

SpeedZone makes your heart pound and your head rip. An aurora of pure energy explodes your own dragster from 0-70mph in three howling seconds. Imagine a Chieftain tank kickstarting your Ferrari at full throttle. Double the impact and you'll be close.

Huge carvings of Confederate legends, Robert E Lee and 'Stonewall' Jackson, breathtakingly blur into life as your helicopter soars past Stone Mountain, the world's largest exposed granite face.

Steep, narrow gorges compress the frantic Chattanooga River, setting for *Deliverance,* into syncopated foam that sucks you one way, then furiously spits you the other. Five Falls, Ravens Rock, and seven-foot white-water rapids draw the last drops of blood from your petrified knuckles.

Sensing a need for respite, Isaac, my giant ebony shuttle-driver recommends shopping. "Take the Marta train to Lennox," he drawls through accordion-like teeth. "They have everything." He is right. Buckhead boasts over 1400 retail outlets centred at Lennox Square Mall.

Four tiers cascade from a crystal atrium to reveal Banana Republic and Brooks Brothers clustered among 240 lively shops anchored by Macy's, Rich's and Neiman Marcus. I note that Harolds, has shoehorned a gleaming red and white Austin Healy into its modest window.

At C. Dickens, salesman Bob Carter proclaims, "A rare set of 11 edition Encyclopaedia Britannica, still garbed in original dust jackets, $6000." "Do you have a first pressing of *GWTW*?" enquires a French voice. Local author, Margaret Mitchell's Civil War creation has just reached 30 million copies, outselling every book except the Bible, with the celluloid version holding the world viewing record.

Perched high above the terraces, Mick's Restaurant with its leisurely service provides a people-watching pinnacle. Declining the giant poached 'Bugs Bunny' carrot, I favour nachos stuffed with cheese and sour cream, decked by a small market garden. Ice cold Coca-Cola, invented in an Atlanta pharmacy over a century ago, is the chosen tipple.

Credit cards and travellers cheques revived, I dodge the Bike Patrol, with their halogen headlights and flashing strobes, to hop the courtesy shuttle for nearby Phipps Plaza.

Here the pace of shopping changes. Saks/Fifth Avenue, Tiffany, Parisian, and Lord & Taylor all help relieve the strain of a bulging wallet. Shopping has only just begun.

There's fashions at Kangaroo Pouch, Buckhead West Village. Brookwood Square offers Calvin Klein, Jenne Maag and Cynthia Rowley. Porcelain at 2300 Peachtree Road and Sculpture in Bennett Street. Fine rugs and Dutch oil paintings hang in Miami Circle and Great Gatsby's displays classic fountains to classic cars.

Taking a breath to check out Virginia-Highland's Art Deco and Marietta Square's crystal, I breeze teapots at Trade Winds, before spying more antiques at Roswell. Moose Breath in Chamblee's completed my heritage collection.

Malls at Peachtree Center, Underground, Cumberland, Northlake, Perimeter, Galleria, North Point, Vinings Jubilee, and Gwinnett Place remain untouched. I cannot even contemplate Outlets.

Getting around is easy. From Five Points hub the modern Marta train reaches out to the city's corners. US$1.50 sees you across town in the comfortable aluminium and black carriages.

At dusk, steamy days evolve into steamy nights. Buckhead is the spot.

Sambuca's jazz makes a good start, followed by a cocktail at Dante's Down The Hatch and a beer in Tongue & Groove. My vibrant tuna salad inspires resident 'starving' oil and canvas artists at Cafe Tu Tu Tango.

Later, Havana beckons, hypnotic Rumba and sweet cigar aroma. Outside, a young drummer forces a familiar tune from simple plastic buckets, backed by a distant Towering Inferno's wail.

Of course, if you want culture there's always the Carter Presidential Center or Martin Luther King Jr's birthplace.

But, in the words immortalised by Scarlett and Reb, "Tomorrow is another day. Frankly my dear, I don't give a damn."

.

# OTHER BOOKS BY THE AUTHOR (Print)

As Good As Gold. ISBN 0-9534818-4-0

Currants, Olives & Cotton. ISBN 99781903467077

De La Rue Straw Hats to Global Securities. ISBN 0- 9534818-2-4
De La Rue: Straw Hats to Global Securities. ISBN 9781903467046

Euro History & Development. ISBN 0-9534818-1-6
Euro: History & Development. ISBN 9781903467053

Holidays 2000. ISBN 0-9534818-7-5

Negotiate to Win! ISBN 0-9534818-6-7

Start Any Business. ISBN 9781903467008

Scripophily. ISBN 0-9534818-5-9
Scripophily. ISBN 9781903467084

Tail-less Cats & Three-Legged Men. ISBN 9781903467091

The Eternal Old Lady. ISBN 0-9534818-3-2
The Eternal Old Lady ISBN 9781903467060

The Green Shoots of Money. ISBN 9781903467107

The Hitmen - Part One. ISBN 0-9534818-8-3

# OTHER BOOKS BY THE AUTHOR (eBook)

As Good As Gold. ISBN 9781903467121

Currants, Olives & Cotton. ISBN 9781903467169

De La Rue. ISBN 9781903467138

Euro. ISBN 9781903467145

Start Any Business. ISBN 9781903467015

Scripophily. ISBN 9781903467176

Tail-less Cats & Three-legged Men. ISBN 9781903467183

The Eternal Old Lady. ISBN 9781903467152

The Green Shoots of Money. ISBN 9781903467114

# NEW EDITIONS & FORTHCOMING BOOKS BY THE AUTHOR

Negotiate to Win! (Print) ISBN 9781903467190
Negotiate to Win! (eBook) ISBN 9781903467206

## ABOUT THE AUTHOR

Ian Moncrief-Scott has over fifty years of broad business experience, mostly gained at international level, based in the UK.

As a former senior executive for a global publishing and information technology company headquartered in the USA, he has contributed to numerous client-facing procurement and outsourcing initiatives worldwide.

Ian has created and participated in numerous small businesses in the UK, Isle of Man and elsewhere.

He has also represented the Isle of Man Government Department for Enterprise in several of its business support schemes. Ian designed and delivered extensive training for its Micro Business Grant Scheme.

In recognition of his long-term service to the Department, Ian was nominated for The Queen's Award for Enterprise Promotion and awarded an official Certificate of Recognition in 2018.

Throughout his career, he has maintained an active interest in start-ups, especially those involving the financial sector.

www.ingramcontent.com/pod-product-compliance
Lightning Source LLC
Chambersburg PA
CBHW071549080526
44588CB00011B/1847